Real Life

GUIDES

CONSTRUCTION

REAL LIFE GUIDES

Practical guides for practical people

In this increasingly sophisticated world the need for manually skilled people to build our homes, cut our hair, fix our boilers and make our cars go is greater than ever. As things progress, so the level of training and competence required of our skilled manual workers increases. In this series of career guides from Trotman, we look in detail at what it takes to train for, get into and be successful at a wide spectrum of practical careers. *Real Life Guides* aim to inform and inspire young people and adults alike by providing comprehensive yet hard-hitting and often blunt information about what it takes to succeed in these careers.

The other titles in the series are:

Real Life Guide: The Armed Forces
Real Life Guide: The Beauty Industry
Real Life Guide: Care
Real Life Guide: Carpentry and Cabinet-Making
Real Life Guide: Catering
Real Life Guide: Construction
Real Life Guide: Distribution and Logistics
Real Life Guide: Electrician
Real Life Guide: The Fire Service
Real Life Guide: Hairdressing
Real Life Guide: Plumbing
Real Life Guide: The Police Force
Real Life Guide: Retailing
Real Life Guide: Transport
Real Life Guide: Working Outdoors
Real Life Guide: Working with Animals and Wildlife
Real Life Guide: Working with Young People

trotman

Real
Life
GUIDES

CONSTRUCTION

Dee Pilgrim

Second edition

Real Life Guide to Construction
This second edition published in 2007 by Trotman
an imprint of Crimson Publishing,
Westminster House, Kew Road, Richmond, Surrey TW9 2ND
www.crimsonpublishing.co.uk

First edition written by Mike Hobbs and published in 2004 by
Trotman and Co Ltd
Reprinted 2005

© Trotman 2004, 2007

Author Dee Pilgrim
Advertising Sarah Talbot, Advertising Sales Director

Designed by XAB

Grateful acknowledgement is made to ConstructionSkills
(formerly Construction Industry Training Board (CITB)) for detailed
training information and permission to reproduce case studies
from their booklet 'A Future in Construction'.

British Library Cataloguing in Publications Data
A catalogue record for this book is available from the British
Library

ISBN 978 1 84455 129 3

Typeset by Mac Style, Nafferton, East Yorkshire
Printed and bound in Great Britain by
Creative Print & Design, Wales

Real Life GUIDES

CONTENTS

About the author

Dee Pilgrim completed the pre-entry, periodical journalism course at the London College of Printing before working on a variety of music and women's titles. She has written numerous articles and interviews for *Company*, *Cosmopolitan*, *New Woman*, *Woman's Journal* and *Weight Watchers* magazines. For many years she covered new output by singer/songwriters for *Top* magazine, which was distributed via Tower Records stores, and during this period interviewed the likes of Tori Amos, Tom Robinson and Joan Armatrading. As a freelancer for Independent Magazines she concentrated on celebrity interviews and film, theatre and restaurant reviews for magazines such as *Ms London*, *Girl About Town*, *LAM* and *Nine to Five*, and in her capacity as a critic she has appeared on both radio and television. She is currently the film reviewer for *Now* magazine and has written a number of titles for Trotman. When not attending film screenings she is active in the Critics' Circle and is the secretary for its film section.

Acknowledgements

Many people helped me put together this book with useful advice but I would like especially to thank the following:

Robert Brown
Tommy Walsh
Neil Smith
Leander Perry

Kathleen Houston
Tim Dindjer
Mina Patria
Anya Wilson

Foreword

CONSTRUCT YOUR FUTURE

If you're looking for a hands-on job that won't keep you cooped up inside then construction is a good bet. While office workers are sweltering in their glass cages, wishing they were out in the sunshine, you will be!

But constriction isn't just one job. It's actually hundreds of them. On big projects like a skyscraper, hotel or office block, you'll have lots of different people who each have their own individual job. Bricklayers, carpenters, scaffolders, plasterers, tillers and loads more besides.

Working in construction you can travel the world (post-work pint in Bondi anyone?), start your own business or even work on a project that could become a national landmark.

City & Guilds are delighted to be part of the Trotman *Real Life Guides* series to help raise your awareness of these vocational qualifications. If an opportunity of involvement in plumbing is for you, City & Guilds has qualifications which will support development throughout your career, helping you to achieve excellence and quality in whatever field you choose.

Introduction

It seems that some people think that working in the construction industry is limiting, but nothing could be further from the truth. There is an enormous variety of jobs connected with the building trade, nearly all demanding skills that you can develop as you go along.

What's more, the industry is constantly growing and renewing itself. It's not recession-proof – no trade is – but there does seem to be a fairly consistent need for building and rebuilding work throughout the UK. According to ConstructionSkills, the Sector Skills Council for the construction industry, between 2007 and 2011 construction in the UK will continue the trend of growth it has enjoyed for the last decade. In 2005, 2.41 million people were employed in construction and that figure is expected to rise to more than 2.8 million by 2011. This means on average 87,600 new construction workers will need to be recruited each year.

We all need to live and work in safe, well-constructed buildings, but the truth is, for a number of years the amount of new homes being built in the UK has fallen far short of demand. In 2003 the government estimated 209,000 new homes needed to be built each year. It has now re-estimated the demand to be for 223,000 new homes each year. This means a mind-boggling 5 million new houses need to be constructed by 2027, great news if you are a bricklayer, roofer, painter, scaffolder, plumber or carpenter.

But it's not just new homes that are in demand: shops, factories and offices need to be properly built and maintained. So do all places that provide essential public services, such as hospitals, libraries and schools, and those offering leisure facilities, such as public swimming pools and recreational centres. Many other large constructions – colleges, universities, shopping malls, surgeries, cinemas, theatres, theme parks, museums, multi-storey car parks, stadiums and so on – require constant updating and rebuilding to meet the needs of the 21st century.

The recent craze in home improvements, illustrated by TV shows such as *Grand Designs* and *Property Ladder*, means many people now want to employ builders to undertake loft extensions, remodel their kitchens, install underfloor heating systems or rip out traditional baths to fit power showers or hot tubs. Finally, major new projects such as the Olympic site and the Manchester Metro link will need the skills of a vast construction workforce in order to be completed on time (read more about the Olympics below).

In the past construction suffered from a poor image and was often not the first choice of career for many young people, especially women and young black and Asian people. However, the perception of the industry is improving as levels of pay and training have risen. Through its national recruitment campaign, Positive Image, ConstructionSkills is promoting construction careers and presenting a more appealing image of the industry to encourage young people to 'make their mark' on the built environment. It has also introduced new training initiatives to get young people interested in a career in construction at an earlier age.

On average 87,600 new construction workers will need to be recruited each year.

The construction industry is a vital pillar of society and has a huge contribution to make to everyone's quality of life. In fact, one of the key issues for the industry is sustainability. While cost is still the main driver for the specification of many projects, a move towards greater sustainability and green building methods and materials is inevitable. In fact, the government is bringing in legislation stating that by 2016 all new homes built in this country must be carbon-neutral – basically they must give out no carbon emissions – this means they will have to be exceedingly energy-efficient. Solar panels, wind turbines, triple glazing, loft insulation, reusing bath water to flush the toilet and the extra plumbing that involves will all become standard features of new homes. At present such homes cost around 40% more to build than ordinary, energy-inefficient houses, but as they are built in bigger numbers they will become cheaper.

By 2016 all new homes built in this country must be carbon-neutral — basically they must give out no carbon emissions.

The UK has a reputation for world-class design, inspirational architecture and high quality building work. It is this country's biggest employer – one in every 14 people works in construction – and it is also the UK's biggest export, generating over £1 billion a year. Over the next five years it is projected that the highest increases in employment will be seen in trade skills, such as bricklayers, and building envelope specialists, such as cladders and roofers (both needing an extra 14% of employees), and wood trade workers, such as carpenters and shopfitters (11%).

In the UK one in every 14 people works in construction.

Equally important are the new professionals and managers needed to enter the industry to oversee this new building work and over 32% of the recruits forecast for the next five years are needed to fill roles such as construction manager, architect or technical staff.

THE OLYMPICS

Although it is not the only major new building project happening across the UK in the next five years, the Olympic park site in Stratford, east London, is by far the most ambitious and important and will employ at least 20,000 new construction workers, although the Mayor of London, Ken Livingstone, puts the number at closer to 50,000. The project has a budget of £9.4 billion including £1.7 billion to regenerate the area and build the infastructure. According to the Olympic Delivery Authority, by 2008 its Demolish, Dig, Design programme will have:

- completed four Tube-sized tunnels, up to 30m deep, enabling the power cables for the Olympics to go underground, thus leading to the demolition of 52 electricity pylons
- installed new water and energy systems including gas, water/sewage, heating/cooking and electricity networks for the site. Planning permission is still being sought for a wind turbine to be constructed at the north end of the site
- regenerated the existing waterways across the park with construction work repairing and replacing 8.5 km of river walls. A new lock and water control system will be installed so barges up to 350 tonnes will have access to the site
- either started or completed a number of new transport links to the site including digging a new deep tunnel for the 'Javelin' train from St Pancras to the park, an extension to the East London Line, and improvements to the Docklands Light Railway, Jubilee Line and Stratford regional station
- built 9,000 new homes and other structures such as the Olympic village, hotels, restaurants and shopping centres in and around the site. Also, the 'Big Four' venues – the actual Olympic stadium, the velodrome (for cycling), the Olympic aquatic centre, and the media centre – will be well into their

construction phases, as will the canoeing centre in Broxbourne and the sailing centre down at Weymouth
- central to helping deliver this project on time are the National Skills Academies for Construction (NSAFC) that deliver project specific training on site. At the Olympic site local people will be offered training to develop their construction skills.

This need for new, well-trained staff and the many developments in construction itself means there has never been a more exciting time for the construction industry. Whether you are working on roads and bridges, or houses and skyscrapers; for a large company or on your own as a local painter and decorator, construction can be a challenging, inspiring and well-paid career choice.

This book is not a construction primer, but it will give you a flavour of the different jobs in the industry to help you decide whether one of them is for you. You'll learn through case studies, examples of a typical working day, job rundowns, quotes and famous examples, so that you can put together a mental picture of life on site.

Your attitude and relevant skills will be tested by a series of quizzes, and you will be able to question your own values to see whether they match those involved in the industry. In short, you will gain every possible insight into construction to determine whether it's the career for you.

You will be able to find out where you can go on training courses, pick up work experience, or have the best chance to nail that elusive first job. You will also find links to websites and the addresses of the industry's governing bodies.

If you're about to leave school or college and are interested in finding out what the construction industry really holds in store, then this book is for you.

TOMMY WALSH

Success story

Be passionate about your chosen career and aim to be the best at what you do.

THE CELEBRITY BUILDER

Tommy Walsh is a familiar face to TV viewers through his many appearances on Ground Force.

The executive producer of the series discovered him when he was doing some building work on her house. Like most overnight success stories, Tommy's was based on years of hard work in his father's hard landscaping business in east London. He now runs the business and brings his 'can do' personality to several TV projects.

Were you always interested in building work as it was the family business?
Yes, and I still am. I love all aspects of it. I drive my wife mad when we're on holiday, because I'm constantly looking up in the air at the local architecture.

What has helped you to progress in your career?
My father was my mentor, and I learned a massive amount from him. Fortunately I also had a healthy enthusiasm for hard work.

Did you do any training apart from learning on the job?
No! I was always propelled by this natural enthusiasm, and an inbuilt curiosity for finding out how things are put together.

Those are essential for proper training on the job, and a determination to make things actually work is the driving force!

What are the best things about your job?
Three things: the camaraderie with all my mates, the consequent wind-ups and, of course, the satisfaction of seeing what you've

I was always propelled by this natural enthusiasm, and an inbuilt curiosity for finding out how things are put together.

done put into action. The wind-ups are too numerous to mention, but if you've seen some of the TV programmes with Alan and Charlie, you'll probably get the general idea.

Conversely, what are the worst things?
Undoubtedly the weather, because working outside in the UK, it's usually so terrible. Do you realise that when I started I was only 5'6" but, with all the rain, I'm now 6'5"…

Have you any advice for school-leavers wishing to enter the industry?
Yes, be passionate about your chosen career and aim to be the best at what you do. You will be given challenging tasks to complete and if you do them well, the job satisfaction (and the rewards) will follow!

Can you identify any qualities that make people more likely to succeed?
Passion about what you do – I can't say it too many times. That is vital, and in my opinion you should also have an ability to learn from your

DID YOU KNOW?

The Imax cinema at the Glasgow Science Centre in Scotland is the first building in the United Kingdom, and only the second in Europe, to be clad in titanium. Its distinctive tower is the only one in the world that can rotate 360 degrees from the ground up. It rotates continually into the face of the wind.

Now is a great time to enter an industry where there is a huge need for dedicated and innovative people.

mentors and other experienced professionals, so be inquisitive, ask relevant questions and listen.

What do you think the future holds for the industry?
Like everything today, the technological advances are creating a truly interesting industry, and an opportunity to enjoy a wonderfully fulfilling career. Now is a great time to enter an industry where there is a huge need for dedicated and innovative people. So why not go ahead?

What's the story?

Your idea of what people do in the construction industry is probably based on the kind of building work you've seen happening, such as the small private builders you watch re-slating roofs, building loft conversions or extensions on private homes, or the hard hat and tabard-wearing construction crews putting up scaffolding or driving dumper trucks around the building site for the new superstore just outside town.

However, this is just the tip of the iceberg because construction covers a myriad of trades and disciplines. There are bricklayers, carpenters, plumbers, electricians, glaziers, architects, site managers, crane operators, engineers and surveyors, to name but a few.

People involved in construction work in a variety of different environments. While builders will be working on site, craftspeople will be in their workshops fabricating different components for the build, and architects will split their time between the office and the site. In fact, the great variety of what is done on different projects in different places is one of the attractions of construction for many people who do not want the normal desk-based 9 to 5 routine.

So it's highly likely that among these many jobs is one to suit you. We will be looking at potential careers in more detail in the Career Opportunities chapter (page 33), but for now here is a rough breakdown of the different work areas in the building trade. Take a look and see which areas interest you most.

PREPARATION

Before work starts on most new buildings, old structures at the site have to be pulled down and a framework erected to enable the builders to work on the new one. That's why **demolition, scaffolding** and **steeplejacking** (that's working on chimneys, steeples, towers or other tall structures) are so important. These are hard, physical and often dangerous jobs where paying attention to what is going on around you is paramount. You have to be fit, strong and have a head for heights for much of this work.

MACHINERY

If you like driving and motor engines, you may find yourself attracted to **plant** and **heavy plant** occupations. Plant is the name given to all the heavy machinery used on site and in mechanical workshops, such as diggers, dumper trucks, cranes, bulldozers and even forklift trucks.

Not only does the industry need people to drive or operate all these machines, it also needs people with the necessary skills to service, repair and maintain them. If you are mechanically minded or interested in science and technology, this part of the industry could be custom-made for your skills.

MANUAL TASKS

One of the areas of the industry with the greatest skills shortage is **wood occupations**. Apparently, an extra 11% of carpenters and joiners will be needed by the industry during the next five years – that's approximately 30,000 new workers. Jobs that involve working with wood include the joiners who make up door frames, windows and staircases, the carpenters who fit these wooden parts into buildings as well as cutting and fitting floorboards and roof timbers, right through to the shopfitters who kit out the banks, shops and restaurants in your local high street.

Apart from being good with their hands, carpenters and joiners need to be good at maths because accuracy is essential in measuring and estimating quantities of materials to be used.

For a more detailed look at carpentry see the *Real Life Guide to Carpentry and Cabinet-Making,* published by Trotman.

PLUMBING

Another area where there is a significant skills shortage is **pipework occupations** – or what we know as plumbing. Plumbers are responsible for ensuring that clean water flows to and from our homes, offices and factories. They are also

An extra 11% of carpenters and joiners will be needed by the industry during the next five years

responsible for the efficient disposal of waste. Wet-only plumbers work just with water, but those who have attended and passed approved courses can also install gas central heating systems, boilers and cookers (gas also travels through pipework). Recently, there has been an influx of eastern European plumbers into the UK, but many of these are unaware of British legislation and do not have the necessary skills to deal with some of the more sophisticated plumbing systems or the new sustainable/renewable plumbing systems, such as solar panels, ground source heat pumps and condensing boilers. According to ConstructionSkills, the UK will need approximately 18,000 fully trained new plumbers during the next five years.

Plumbing is detailed, often intricate work, so if you like doing fiddly things and don't mind getting dirty, this could be for you. Again, for a more detailed look at pipework occupations, see the *Real Life Guide to Plumbing,* published by Trotman.

STONES AND SLATES

Although they are not the only materials used in modern buildings, brick and stone probably spring to mind quickly when you think about construction. The work of the **bricklayer** and the **stonemason** not only involves the general construction of a building, but also often entails more creative work, such as decorative borders or designs. Once again, this is a job for someone who is good with their hands and is fit and strong. A lot of work is done high above the ground, so you also have to be comfortable with heights.

This is especially true if you decide to go into **roofing**. If you'd like a job with a view, you could opt for being a traditional roof tiler and slater, or you could work with one of the newer roofing materials, such as liquid waterproofing. Either way you are going to be out in all weathers and at all heights, so those who get dizzy on the first floor need not apply.

FINISHING

There is also a skills shortage in **finishing occupations**, such as plastering, suspended ceiling fixing and dry lining. In fact, ConstructionSkills estimates a further 13% of such skilled workers will be needed in the next five years. While the plasterer works with wet plaster to give either a smooth or textured finish to walls and ceilings, a dry liner works with plasterboard or wallboard panels. Suspended ceiling fixers usually work on large

If you'd like a job with a view, you could opt for being a traditional roof tiler and slater.

modern structures, such as office blocks or hospitals, where the ceilings conceal air-conditioning pipes, fire protection systems and electrical cabling.

Because the work that finishers do can be seen when construction is completed, they need to pay attention to detail and be good with their hands.

All the above are commonly known as crafts skills, but that isn't the whole story in construction. As we become more environmentally aware and opt for greener solutions to our energy needs, newly trained construction workers who specialise in installing energy-saving technology (solar panels, heat sumps, grey water systems, wind turbines, wall, roof and underfloor insulation) will be much in demand. This is also true of construction workers trained in heritage skills, such as thatchers and dry stone wallers.

SUPPORT ROLES

Just as important as the people with craft skills are people who work in technical support.

Traditionally, the craft skills have been learned by young people apprenticing themselves to older workers who then teach them the skills 'on the job'.

Jobs in this area are for people with excellent communication and supervision skills who need to have detailed knowledge of construction law. They include estimators who work out the costs of a build, building service technicians who make sure systems such as heating, air-conditioning, plumbing, electricity, gas, telephone and, increasingly, computer cabling are installed efficiently and accurately, and civil engineering technicians who produce detailed drawings for projects as diverse as roads, reservoirs, bridges and tunnels. If you are a whizz with computer systems this may well be for you as many technical support staff use CAD (computer-aided design) to produce technical drawings. It is also helpful to be good at maths and measuring.

MANAGEMENT

The technical support staff are usually the bridge between the crafts people and the **managerial** and **professional** positions – such as the architects, structural engineers, surveyors, construction managers and quantity surveyors – and they are essential to the construction industry. They all need good leadership and communication skills and must be prepared to take on a high level of responsibility. If you don't like the stress of being in charge and having to make decisions, these positions may not be your cup of tea.

Obviously, because of the specialised nature of these roles, most managerial or professional positions entail intense and sometimes lengthy training before you can become qualified.

As you can see, there's more to construction than first meets the eye. From that initial architectural drawing to the final laying of floorboards and lick of paint, a whole host of different skills are needed.

Traditionally, the craft skills have been learned by young people apprenticing themselves to older workers who then teach them the skills 'on the job'. This is still the case with many of the professions mentioned above, but not all.

But before we look at training, you'll need to know if you have the right skills, strengths and talents to become a part of this industry. In the next chapter we discuss what you can bring to the building business and what you will need to succeed in it.

DID YOU KNOW?

Heathrow's new Terminal 5 is the largest free-standing building in the UK, costing £4.3 billion to construct. 30,000 sq m of glass façade have been installed in the 40m high building and the 18,500–tonne single span roof took over 11 months to lift into place. It is due to open in March 2008.

Tools of the trade

3

Before listing the specific skills and disciplines required in construction, it's a good idea to look at the skills, attitudes and abilities that you will need, as a general rule, in order to be successful in the industry. These are the tools that might make the difference between getting your desired job or just missing out.

To get on in just about any aspect of the business, you have to be good at working with your hands.

STRENGTHS AND SKILLS

Building sites are dangerous places. Heavy plant will be moving loads of building materials around. There will be people working on scaffolding. Cranes will be working high above you. That is why being totally aware of what is going on around you is imperative for your own and for others' safety.

Health and safety regulations at all sites where construction takes place are very stringent, and rightly so. A momentary lapse in concentration could result in serious injury or even death. That is why, whatever area of construction you decide to go into, there will be a specific unit or units of training dedicated to health and safety (everything from the correct use of equipment, such as safety goggles and gloves, to how to lift heavy loads without damaging your back). If you are a person who can pay meticulous attention to these rules, you will ensure your own safety and that of your workmates.

It may seem obvious, but it really is true that to get on in just about any aspect of the business, you have to be good at **working with your hands**. There are all sorts of exercises you can do to improve your hand-to-eye co-ordination, but usually there has to be a certain amount of natural talent for you to build on. Other indicators that show you might have the right manual skills are a good aptitude for DIY work around the house, an ability to carry out handyman and electrical repair work, and a deft touch leading to 'green fingers' in the garden or on the allotment. If you feel that you could improve the work you do with your hands, try refining your skills by doing some odd jobs in preparation, or take a class at school such as woodworking or metalworking.

Your **vision** needs to be clear because there are all sorts of tiny errors that can creep in if you're not being vigilant. It's obviously vital that these are put right immediately, because any mistakes made early on can be magnified as construction work progresses. By the same token, you must be able to retain a sense of balance and perspective to ensure that the work you are doing is in harmony with the whole project. If you think your vision is impaired, check with an optician and wear glasses or contact lenses if required.

When you're working on any site, for much of the time you will have to be reliant on the skills of others – and they'll have to rely on you. As a consequence, it is important that you are good at **working in a team**. If you are happy to be a team player and like the camaraderie of working with others, then you will be well suited for a career in construction.

Although not all the work in construction requires you to be **agile**, if you're going to be working on site the chances are you'll need to do a lot of moving around. So you should have the sort of body that is highly flexible, with limbs and muscles that don't seize up at the first physical challenge.

Natural fitness is therefore important and if you feel yours needs improvement, you can always increase your suppleness by working out at the gym or taking part in a sport or other exercise that you enjoy. In fact, if you're hoping to work in any manual job in the industry, then being physically fit and having **good upper body strength** is a distinct advantage. It will also help you to avoid injury, although some wear and tear on your body is inevitable in most construction sectors. For instance, many carpenters find they suffer from bad backs as they age (all that bending over, cutting, planing and fixing), while many plumbers get arthritis in their knees from kneeling down fitting pipes together. Many of the tasks involved in the construction industry are physically demanding because a lot of the equipment is heavy and you'll be on the go for quite long periods.

Being able to **communicate** well with people is vital. You need good listening skills to really understand what it is that your colleagues and supervisors are telling you, because often you will have to act rapidly on what they're saying. Good communication is the secret of working together well as a team and you must also be able to put your points across clearly. If you're working for yourself or are in charge of a job, you must also be able to explain very clearly to clients what exactly it is that you're going to do (or have done) and how much it's going to cost. Tied in

If you're hoping to work in any manual job in the industry, then being physically fit and having good upper body strength is a distinct advantage.

with this is being literate; that is, being able to communicate by the written word clearly and precisely. You may have to write a report or tender a written quote for a job.

Being **reliable** and making sure you're always in a position to do what you say you are going to do is an absolute must. When you're working for other people, you have an obligation to them to carry out the work so that they can deal with clients confidently. If you're in business for yourself, you owe a duty of care to your own clients to fulfil every part of the job reliably.

Punctuality is a key part of reliability. These days time really is money and if you are late, it could well mean that other members of your team will have to wait until your work has been completed before they can do their own jobs. This is how projects miss their finishing deadlines and go over budget, so make sure your timekeeping is good. Also, as you'll read elsewhere in this book, in the summer work on building sites tends to start very early in the morning in order to make the most of the daylight hours, so it's no good snoozing away in bed; your employer needs you out there on the job. If you are going to be late for some reason, contact the people who matter (your boss or your client) to let them know.

All aspects of education are clearly helpful to you in your career, but if there's any one subject that you are likely to use a lot, you'll find it is **mathematics**. Whether you're working out angles, putting together a schedule of supplies you'll need for the job or calculating your wages, good attention to your maths studies at school and college is bound to add up in your favour. It'll be of great practical value. For instance, think of the complicated maths a carpenter needs to do in order to work out all the angles of a curved wooden staircase.

In addition to maths skills, anyone who aspires to a job in construction should have a sound knowledge of the basic principles of **chemistry** and **physics** – and if you want to get involved in some of the design and engineering jobs on the creative side of the industry, you'll have to take your understanding of theory and practice to a much higher level.

Do not underestimate the personal qualities of **trustworthiness** and **honesty**. You will often be working alone in clients' homes or premises, and they will all need to be absolutely reassured that they can leave you to work unsupervised. You must, therefore, be able to inspire their trust. Provide references if possible, and become a member of a recognised industry association, such as the Institute of Plumbers and Heating Engineers (IPHE). Don't just have a mobile phone number, but give people an address and landline number as well and generally do everything you can to prove yourself worthy of their trust. Properly designed and printed business cards show you have a professional attitude to what you do.

Just about every job you'll do in construction requires you to travel quickly from A to B so you really must **learn to drive**. Once you're working on your own, your ability to drive will be crucial – and if you are going to work with heavy plant, it is essential. People may joke about 'white van man' but getting new baths, radiators, window frames and bricks to the site is an essential part of the job and if you are self-employed you can make good use of your 'white van' by advertising your business telephone number on its sides.

In addition to physical stamina, it's important that you have the **mental stamina** to be able to cope with working in a high-pressure environment. As you move up the career ladder, you may well become responsible for overseeing the work of other people and this responsibility can prove stressful. If you are new to working life, taking exams may be the only direct experience you have of being under pressure. That is why getting some work experience is essential. Why not get a Saturday job working in a building supplier's shop or a timber yard? It's a great way of learning to interact with other people, both fellow workers and the public.

A lot of construction work is painstaking and delicate (cutting precise joints in carpentry, or fitting together narrow pipework under a bathroom sink if you are a plumber) and it requires a great deal of **patience**. You may be engaged in a particularly tricky aspect of building work, or the weather may be conspiring to put you behind schedule. However, you should always take your time and make sure you get things right because rectifying mistakes can prove to be more time-consuming than doing the job perfectly in the first place.

One thing that is essential is to take **pride** in your completed work. No matter how much you feel you're under pressure to finish the job in a certain time, you must still ensure that everything is made ready in perfect working order, without cutting corners. Each client needs to know that the job has been carried out to the best of your ability. Any attempt to skim over the work is a false economy at best, and can be downright counter-productive at worst. All of the people interviewed for this book talked about the pride and satisfaction they feel on successfully completing a job. It's one of the main reasons why they like what they do.

Learn to keep your cool and be **polite** at all times. However unreasonable your boss or client may be, keep your temper and

People in the industry are professional and know that doing their tasks to the best of their ability comes first.

explain everything clearly and logically. This is especially true if you are a self-employed builder, carpenter or plumber dealing directly with members of the public. If your clients find you to be polite, they will be more likely to recommend you to others. Never underestimate the economic benefits of good word of mouth!

Because working on site (and being connected with the trade in any way) needs such good teamwork, you'll discover that having a good **sense of humour** is a great advantage. Sometimes, when things have gone wrong (as they invariably do in any walk of life), it's an absolute necessity.

People involved in the building trade usually have a fund of jokes and good stories. Generally, though, the time to make light of things is after you've sorted out any problems that have arisen. People in the industry are professional and know that doing their tasks to the best of their ability comes first. Clients are apt not to see the funny side of things if there's potential for disaster.

You must have the **ability to adapt** to different and changing circumstances.

No two jobs are exactly the same and you have to be willing to learn about new aspects of your work all the time. This is particularly true if you're working for yourself or are in charge of a team. People are late, become ill and get called away all the time and it'll be up to you to adapt schedules and working priorities to complete the job on time.

Increasingly, being computer-literate is a must-have skill if you want to get on in the construction trades. This is because so many plans are drawn up by CAD and if modifications need to be made, they will be made on a computer. If you are a self-employed builder it pays to look professional and keep all your client files on computer so invoices can be sent out punctually and correspondence and estimates can be printed off.

POSSIBLE PROBLEM AREAS

There are some physical and mental conditions that could hold you back. Think about the following points seriously before deciding whether this really is the industry for you.

Construction workers use harsh chemicals on an almost daily basis, everything from paints and solvents to resins, adhesives and varnishes. These can cause difficulties if you have **skin allergies or respiratory problems**, such as contact dermatitis or asthma. The fumes and smell from paint, the dust from bricks and rubble, even the possibility of toxic poisoning can all affect you on site. This is why there is such an emphasis on safety gear such as face masks, goggles and heavy duty gloves. However, even when used properly they cannot guarantee 100% protection.

There are several sprays, pills and other treatments on the market to help you cope with such a condition, but it is only fair to warn you that being in close contact with these chemicals and dust might exacerbate any problems you have. Carry any alleviating sprays or medication with you wherever you go.

Because of all the lifting and bending down and straightening up builders have to do, bad backs are part of the territory. If you have a family history of back problems you may need to consider jobs within the industry that involve less manual labour. Again, many plumbers complain of arthritis in their knees and if you know your family is prone to arthritic joints you may be better suited to a desk job.

Most building work takes place either outdoors or in relatively open spaces, but occasionally you might have to work in narrow basements or cellars and if you suffer from **claustrophobia**, you're going to have difficulties. This fear of confined spaces can arise either from physical or mental causes. In both cases it can be treated, but you will need some specialist advice to determine exactly what the cause is.

If you're working as part of a team, you'll find out very rapidly that everyone will expect you to be well organised. **Poor organisation** can really cause teamwork to suffer and the last thing you'll want is to let down your colleagues. If you come to set up your own business and you're no good at organising yourself, then you're going to have to learn fast.

The flipside of punctuality is **poor timekeeping** and if you're someone who seems chronically unable to turn up anywhere on time, then it's a problem you're going to have to solve very quickly. Nobody minds someone being late for a good reason, as long as it doesn't happen too often and is explained in a phone call, but when it occurs regularly, it becomes impolite to your clients and colleagues and contributes to you being regarded as unreliable and unprofessional.

Some construction jobs will require you either to work outside or at heights, maybe on roofs. If you suffer from **vertigo**, you should be aware that this could cause you some distress. There are various treatments available to ease this condition but, as with claustrophobia and breathing difficulties, it may also affect your ability to do the work properly. The problem is not as acute for most people in the industry as for, say, a scaffolder or steeplejack, where a fear of heights probably rules you out as a candidate for employment.

One downside of construction you might not have thought about is that sometimes the **work is not done in normal hours**. This is usually not true of the self-employed builder who is working in people's homes, but is true of employees of large construction firms working to tight and stringent deadlines.

Often it is written into the contract that if the work is not successfully completed by a certain date then financial penalties will come into play (usually in the form of bonuses not being paid). Because of this there is often a time consideration built into the job, so that if it looks like the completion date will be missed, the workers will have to work longer hours in order to complete on time.

Also, construction work tends to take seasonal variations into account. As stated before, summer days have more hours of daylight than winter days, so work during the summer may start at sun up and continue until sun down. This means you could be on site from six in the morning until late into the evening, so you may find yourself missing out on evenings spent with friends – a consideration if an active social life is important to you.

Finally, larger construction projects will often require construction workers to be on site at weekends as well as during the week, so bang goes that friendly game of footie or trip to the gym you had planned for Saturday afternoon. If you don't like the hours you work being disrupted, this may not be for you.

IS CONSTRUCTION FOR YOU?

By now you should have a better idea of whether you are really suited to a career in construction.

If you are still convinced the building trade is for you, then the short quiz opposite will quickly show how suitable a candidate you are. Just say whether you think each statement is true or false.

I like to see the results of my work immediately
TRUE/FALSE

Working in construction means less communication with other people
TRUE/FALSE

Customer service doesn't matter if I'm not in charge of a project
TRUE/FALSE

It's worth cutting corners to get things done more quickly
TRUE/FALSE

Teamwork doesn't matter when I'm the only one on site
TRUE/FALSE

Working with my hands doesn't give me any satisfaction
TRUE/FALSE

I need to work in the same controlled environment each day
TRUE/FALSE

If you have answered FALSE to all or most of these, you've probably got the right attitude to succeed in construction.

If you have answered TRUE to all or most statements, you might not really want to work on site. Have you considered administration or support functions?

If your answers are fairly evenly split, you need to think carefully about what you're really looking for in a career.

4

Case study 1

> I love solving problems and finding solutions...the most satisfaction I get is from seeing even a minor project through from an idea to completion.

It was almost inevitable building would be involved in Robert's career as his family history is steeped in construction. He started out as a general painter/decorator and then trained to be a building surveyor as a mature student. He is now the New Works Manager (Building Surveyor) at Interserve.

How did you get your first job – and what was it?

Instead of doing an official apprenticeship, I worked with a guy who was a professional painter and decorator and he showed me the ropes. The advantage to that was that he was a perfectionist, so he taught me how to do everything correctly. From there I progressed to managing my own team undertaking smallish domestic works, and it was while working on a very expensive property some years later that the owner handed me the structural survey of the building to look over. I realised I could analyse the survey and pinpoint problem areas. I decided to go to South Bank University and studied for a BSc in Building Surveying. The course was three years full-time, but I split it up to do it over five years, part-time, so I could go out into the industry and gain experience. During that time I worked for a top building surveying consultancy and learned contract adminsitration and management, and I feel very lucky to have had that opportunity.

Describe what you do now.
Interserve plc is a large company and one of its contracts is for the Metropolitan Police Area South. Basically, I go into their buildings and sort out any structural problems they may have. I can be looking at something very small, such as broken hinges, to major cracks in walls. For instance, I was recently called in to inspect a flat roof on a building which was leaking. I advise and consult on whether the buildings conform to building regulations and health and safety regulations, and that means I write lots of reports. However, half the time what I do is to put people's minds to rest. I also project manage where I advise on costs and see the project through to completion.

What are the best things (and the worst) about your job?
I love the variety of what I do. Visiting different sites is fun and it means you get to meet a lot of new people. I love solving problems and finding solutions. Even putting people's minds to rest is nice, but the most satisfaction I get is from seeing even a minor project through from an idea to completion.

The only downside is the pressure you are under because if you get something wrong it could potentially be very serious.

You have to have good communication skills and the ability to talk to people on all levels, from the client, to the builder, to the structural engineer.

How do you see your career progressing?
I'm incorporated into the Chartered Institute of Building (CIOB) and I want to go on and get my full membership. That will be

recognition of my professional competence and will mean sitting an assessment of professional competence (APC). But it doesn't really stop there. Within the built environment it is a process of continual professional development because if you stand still you will be left behind; legislation changes all the time and so you have to keep on top of things. In order to do that I subscribe to *Building* magazine.

Can you identify any qualities that make people more likely to succeed?
You have to have good communication skills and the ability to talk to people on all levels, from the client, to the builder, to the structural engineer. You need a head for figures, but it is even more essential to be literate because you will be writing a lot of reports and you may have to write in a number of styles. To do what I do you have to have an interest in buildings and architecture and have a thirst for knowledge and enthusiasm.

What would be your best piece of advice for people wanting to do what you do?
Go and work on a building site for a while or get a holiday job working in the industry. If you get some experience at the sharp end of the construction trade you'll be able to see how difficult it can really be.

FAQs

Now we've looked at whether you are suited to a career in construction, there may be some questions you need answered before making up your mind. Things like levels of pay, opportunities for advancement and the possibility of becoming more highly qualified could influence your decision.

Here are some of the most commonly asked questions about working in construction. The answers should give you a better idea if this is truly for you.

HOW LONG DO I HAVE TO TRAIN FOR?

There is no set length of training because, on the one hand, you can choose to take the qualifications at whatever speed you wish and, on the other hand, it depends on how far up the levels of qualification you wish to go. However, if you're considering trying to pass the NVQ level 1 or 2, it should take two to three years, and progressing to level 3 should take a further year to 18 months. Training for such qualifications is discussed in detail in the Training chapter (page 42).

WHAT'S THE PAY LIKE?

Good. You'll be paid at rates agreed by the Building and Allied Trades Joint Industrial Council (BATJIC) for the industry. In March 2007, the BATJIC came to a memorable agreement with the construction unions when it broke the £10 per hour barrier for key workers for the first time. Until March 2008 the rates were set at: £10.06 an hour for craft operatives with NVQ level 3 (£392.34 per 39-hour week), £8.65 an hour for craft operatives with NVQ level 2 (£337.35 per 39-hour week) and £7.40 an hour for general operatives (£288.60 per 39-hour week). Obviously, apprentices will earn less than this but will be learning as they earn.

WILL I HAVE A NORMAL WORKING WEEK?

Yes, you usually do, varying from eight to ten hours each day at the normal times, depending on the terms of your contract. Site work tends to last ten hours, whereas some supporting office jobs require eight hours a day. As discussed in the Tools of the Trade chapter (page 15), construction workers tend to make the most of the longer days during the summer months by working

Many of the skills that you learn in the industry are readily transferable, and several would enable you to set up in business for yourself straight away.

longer hours. You may, of course, get a chance to work overtime on various projects, in which case you could earn considerably more for the longer hours.

WHAT ABOUT HOLIDAYS?

Holidays are fairly standard, offering on average four working weeks each year, as well as all the public holidays (Christmas, New Year, Easter, bank holidays). Many companies will also offer extra days as holiday depending on length of service, so your entitlement may rise to five weeks, or above, the longer you stay with the same employer. If you end up working for yourself, one of the great advantages is that you can choose your own holiday arrangements.

CAN I CHANGE CAREERS EASILY?

Yes, you can. As you will have discovered, many of the skills that you learn in the industry are readily transferable, and several would enable you to set up in business for yourself straight away, such as work that you've done as a glazier, a painter and decorator, a carpenter and joiner, or a plumber. At the other end of the spectrum, if you have qualified as an engineer, you can always consider moving from construction to industries where your skills would be relevant, such as building motor vehicles.

CAN I WORK ABROAD?

You are permitted to work in any country that is a member of the European Union (although obviously being able to speak the relevant foreign language will help). If you want to try this out, there is a Young Workers' Exchange Programme (for 18 to 28 year olds) which will give you work experience or training in the country of your choice for as little as three weeks or up to 16 months. There are no such guarantees for other parts of the world, but if you have some solid qualifications behind you, that should stand you in good stead.

WHAT ARE THE PROSPECTS FOR PROMOTION?

Promotion prospects are very good indeed within all the areas of the industry. Obviously a great deal, if not all, depends on you. If you work and study hard, complete your training swiftly, develop your expertise and show willingness to do more than is necessary, you'll get on just fine. There's also a possibility that you may want to start up in business for yourself.

WILL I GET HELP IF I WANT TO BECOME MY OWN BOSS?

Yes, there are several booklets and courses available to help you prepare for the various facets of setting up your own company.

DID YOU KNOW?

At present there are 24 million homes in Britain, but with demand outstripping supply many more are needed (government estimates say 5 million new homes will be needed by 2027). A report by the Sustainable Development Commission (SDC) estimates that homes built from 2007 onwards will make up one quarter of Britain's housing by 2050.

WHAT DOES THE PUBLIC THINK OF THE INDUSTRY?

It varies. On the one hand, British construction is said to have a very good standing in the world, and that reputation has been earned by some consistently good work on high-profile projects. On the other hand, many individuals have had bad experiences from employing rogue builders and consequently have rather negative things to say.

Generally, these botched jobs have happened at the lower end of the scale, but it will be up to you (and people like you) to change these perceptions.

WHAT WILL I GET OUT OF IT APART FROM A CAREER?

Three main things – a strong feeling of satisfaction and self-worth, a chance to meet a broad cross-section of people, and the knowledge that you won't have to look far to get your own building work carried out.

You'll feel satisfied because you are able to help people by putting together something built to last. To be able to take part in a major construction project, or several smaller ones, will give you a powerful sense of self-worth.

Furthermore, you are very likely to meet many different people. As in the rest of life, you probably won't want to be friends with them all, but communicating with each and every one of them will be interesting on many different levels.

6

Career opportunities

In the What's The Story? chapter (page 9), we looked at the kind of jobs available in the construction industry. As you saw, there are so many different things you can do in the building trade that there is bound to be something to suit you and your own unique abilities.

We now look in more detail at the different areas of construction work and the huge variety of careers in each area.

DEMOLITION, SCAFFOLDING, STEEPLEJACK

If you're interested in cutting things down and blowing up buildings, then you'd be a good bet to become a **demolition operative**, but you'll need to be acutely safety-conscious as well. According to figures for 2006 from the Office of National Statistics there are 2,570 demolition and wrecking companies operating in the UK, employing 22,000 workers.

If you really love heights, then there is always the chance of finding work as a **steeplejack** to repair and maintain tall, exposed structures, and there are plenty of jobs as a **scaffolder** available to make the tasks of other construction workers easier. Or you might find work as a **steel erector**, putting up the steel frames of industrial or multi-storey buildings.

PLANT

To ensure that everything is running properly, all sites need a **plant mechanic** to maintain and repair the equipment. Or if you've ever fancied driving a crane on site, or maybe shifting earth or steering a forklift truck, you can apply to be a **plant operator**.

Most equipment on site is rented from plant hire companies rather than owned, so ensuring that it's readily available is the task of the **plant hire controller**. However, someone needs to negotiate the hire and sale of that equipment in the first place – the **plant sales representative**. Apparently, there are 23,000 people involved in the renting and operation of construction equipment in the UK.

WORKING WITH WOOD
According to the Office for National Statistics there are over 272,000 carpenters and joiners in this country and over 21,000 joinery firms, and with construction now starting on the Olympic site, ConstructionSkills estimates 11% more wood trade workers will be needed over the next five years, so now is a great time to start training. If you want to be a **carpenter** and **joiner**, you'll have to work on all the initial and later fittings of timber materials in each building. On site **formworkers** make the temporary structures to hold the wet concrete before it sets, **first fix carpenters** finish off the internal woodwork and **second fix carpenters** complete the final wood fixtures, such as skirting boards.

Meanwhile, in machine shops, **machinists** prepare and shape all the floorboards, roofing timbers and wood panels to be used in construction.

ROOFING
If you're keen on applying the layers of felt to roofs to make a solid waterproof surface, you could apply to be a **built-up felt roofer**. Similarly, the **mastic asphalter** works on roofs and floors with large surface areas to make them waterproof. And the job of a **roof sheeter** and **cladder** is to fix the outer layers onto very large buildings, normally industrial or retail, to keep out water.

There is still call for the **roof slater** and **tiler** (in fact there are 50,000 of them in the UK) to work on slates and tiles, usually for houses or repairing older buildings. Flat roofs often use advanced single-ply materials to perform the same function – fixing them is the job of a **single-ply roofer**. A **lead sheeter** has to use the material for waterproof flashings, often where the roofing has some decorative element.

ConstructionSkills has highlighted building envelope specialist (cladders and roofers) as one of the key areas where more trained workers are needed, so now is a great time to enter this profession.

TROWEL

There are approximately 87,000 bricklayers and masons currently working in the UK and ConstructionSkills says bricklaying will see a 14% rise in employment in the next five years. The job of a **bricklayer** is to build the inside and outside walls and archways with bricks and blocks. The preparation of the site for work is the chief purpose of a **construction operative**, sometimes called a groundworker.

If you're fascinated by sculpting, you could look for work as a **stonemason**, either working off site (**banker mason**) or fixing the finished articles on site (**fixer mason**). Because Britain has so many fine heritage buildings made of stone, there is a real call for the skills of the **craft mason**, restoring and replacing crumbling masonry on anything from Tudor palaces to the country's many cathedrals.

The person who applies the final finish – known as a render – to the outside walls of buildings is called a **renderer**. Similar to a renderer, the job of the **plasterer** is mainly to apply plaster to inside walls, either on new buildings or repairing old ones. The talents of the skilled plasterer are much in demand, especially those who can achieve the more decorative plaster finishes. The number of plasterers has remained pretty stable at 13,000 for the past four years.

INTERIORS AND FINISHING

In larger buildings, there is often a need to attach ceiling panels to the floors above, which falls to the **ceiling fixer**. Linked to this is the work of a **dryliner (fixer)** who puts up internal partitions to serve as ceiling and wall surfaces. As the name suggests, the **dryliner (finisher)** brings these surfaces to a good, clean state ready for final decorating.

Self-evidently, the role of a **floor layer** is to ensure that all buildings involved have clean, level floors. The job of a **glazier** is to cut and fix all glass for windows, doors, some surfaces and roof skylights. There are approximately 6,000 companies delivering floor and wall covering services in the UK, employing 23,000 people.

If you're keen on painting, you could consider applying to be a **painter** and **decorator**, working on both interiors and exteriors. In the layout of some offices, there is a need for a **partitioning (relocatable) fixer** to divide up large spaces. Obviously tiles are not confined to roofs, and you can specialise for work indoors as a **wall** and **floor tiler**.

TECHNICAL SUPPORT

If the manual side of the construction trade does not interest you, then there are plenty of roles for the more academically minded. In fact, as previously stated, ConstructionSkills is predicting that the UK will need 32% more recruits in roles such as construction manager, architect and other technical staff in the next five years. Here are just a few for you to consider.

There are many construction materials needed for each job, and getting hold of them is the responsibility of the **buyer**. Before that happens, the **estimator** has to work out how much the project will cost to tender for the contract. Once the work has been won, the **quantity surveyor (contractor)** monitors its progress and checks that the budget isn't exceeded. On the other hand, the **quantity surveyor (private)** checks the project's progress on behalf of the client company.

Once the work has commenced, it is the responsibility of the **site engineer** to see that it is completed safely and accurately.

All construction work needs precise drawings as a starting point, often done by a **CAD operative.** Putting up the structures needs a lot of organisation and supervision, carried out by a **building technical support** team. Large-scale construction projects (motorways, runways, bridges, etc.) are backed by a **civil engineering technical support** team. Getting equipment on site for large projects is the job of the **plant** and **engineering technical support** team. And even specialist roofers need the scheduling and organisation of a **roofing technical support** team.

All surveyors on large projects have the backing of a **surveying technical support** team. Again, everyone working on a large construction site is underpinned by a **site technical support** team. Finally, quality control on construction projects is maintained by the **site inspector**, and the **planner** ensures that everything is organised to be completed on schedule.

A **building control surveyor** makes sure building regulations and other legislation are followed in the design and construction stages of new or altered buildings.

Helping to protect the UK's building heritage is the **building conservation officer**, who is responsible for historic buildings such as lighthouses, windmills, churches, country houses and even our manufacturing heritage such as mills and factories.

He/she applies for grants for restoration, writes reports and inspects the buildings. Most building conservation officers work alone.

DESIGN, ENGINEERING, FINANCIAL, MANAGEMENT AND PLANNING

All construction or refurbishment projects start with the practical ideas of an **architect** who draws up plans and designs. Support for architects comes from an **architectural technologist** who ensures that their designs are technically sound.

The job of a **building services engineer** is to install all the utilities that buildings need to function properly. All existing buildings need maintenance and repair, which is the chief task of a **building surveyor**. When buildings are renovated or valued, the project is planned by a **general practice surveyor**.

The monitoring of the running costs of a project is carried out by a **quantity surveyor**. Each site (or section of a site if it's a very large project) is run by a **construction manager**, sometimes called a **site manager** or an **agent**. A **structural engineer** assesses whether standing structures (such as bridges) can continue to operate safely and new projects enlist one from the start.

If you're interested in devising the whole urban (and rural) environment, you can aim to be a **town (and country) planner**. Major design projects, such as those for highways, harbours and airports, are the responsibility of a **civil engineer**. The design of these major projects (such as bridges, railways and dams) is carried out by a **civil engineering designer**.

As soon as a large building has been occupied, its upkeep becomes the responsibility of a **facilities manager**, while its conformity to health and safety regulations and other legal aspects is overseen by a **building control officer**.

A **geospacial modeller** produces computerised 3-D models of natural and built landscapes in order to help plan construction projects.

In order to know how each project might affect the marine environment (or be affected by it), reports are drawn up by a **hydrographic surveyor**. A **land surveyor** measures and records landscape features to produce models and maps for construction projects and information. The quality of the outdoor spaces that surround us is the province of the **landscape architect**.

As the name implies, a **project manager** monitors the planning, management, co-ordination and financial control of a construction project.

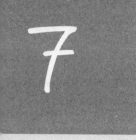

7

HOLLY BENNETT
Case study 2

It's hard physical work but it's always interesting and often a lot of fun. No two jobs are the same, which is something I really like about the work.

Holly Bennett is a Demolition Site Manager, working for Controlled Demolition Group Ltd. She qualified from an Institute of Explosive Engineers 'Shot Firing in Construction' course with an EPIC Shot Firing Certificate.

'I joined the company originally to do administrative support work in their head office as an office junior. My plan was to go on to study law at college and become a solicitor. However, I sometimes used to have to go to sites where the company was working and a lot of the demolition work looked really exciting. So I changed my mind and went to study shot firing at college at the same time as doing all the practical side of the course on site with the company. It went really well.

'Now that I've qualified, in my current job I go to different sites, check on health and safety issues, make sure everyone is working properly, that the pre-weakening is done and that the job is running smoothly. Then we do our bit. It's hard physical work but it's always interesting and often a lot of fun.

'The end result is spectacular. No two jobs are the same, which is something I really like about the work.

'You've certainly got to have a good head for heights. So far, the highest chimney I've had to do was 800 ft and I had to climb up to 400 ft to place charges. That was probably the most spectacular of the lot.

'I also like to travel and I've already been to Ireland, Norway, Morocco and Florida in the USA to work, as well as going to just about every part of the UK.

'I'm the only woman on site, which was sometimes difficult at first, because I'm also in charge of the team. However, that's become much less of an issue since I know them all so well now – and the good thing is that we get along fine and it works.'

DID YOU KNOW?

In 2006, housebuilder BOVIS saw its pre-tax profits soar by 14% to £132 million after it sold 3,123 homes, 400 more than expected. The £1.4 billion company is a frontrunner to build much of the housing for the 2012 Olympic village.

Training

The ways in which you can train for a career in construction are almost as many and varied as the types of jobs in the industry, so finding something to suit you can seem complicated. Don't panic! It is actually quite straightforward.

There are three main routes into the industry, each providing you with just the right amount of training and vocational qualifications for the job you choose. However, one of the best things about the construction industry is that you don't need to follow the paths set out below. Once you've started training, you can move your career path in different directions by gaining further qualifications.

CRAFTSPEOPLE

Most people train and gain qualifications as they work, although there are other kinds of training schemes. You'll be learning while working and also attending college on a day release or block release basis. To enter the industry as a trainee craftsperson, you will need a good basic education including maths and English. Craftspeople are creative and will learn skills that involve using their hands but they will also have the chance to achieve qualifications that can take them to technician or management positions.

TECHNICIANS

To be a technician you'll need four good GCSE passes, A-levels or a vocational college qualification. There are two main options: either you can work and go to college part-time or you can get full-time qualifications at college before joining the industry. The work is demanding and, if you wish, you can use the qualifications you gain at this level to go to university in the future.

GRADUATES

If you have a university degree (usually in a relevant subject such as civil and structural engineering), you can expect a high level of responsibility when you enter the profession. You will be trained for highly specialised or management positions and will have the opportunity to gain professional qualifications, such as chartered status. If you are not a graduate but wish to move on in the profession, you can take a foundation degree, which most people do after achieving other qualifications, such as NVQs. They mix vocational and academic learning and can be studied part-time or full-time. Depending on how much time a week you spend on your studies, a Foundation Degree should take between two and three years to complete.

APPRENTICESHIPS

One of the best and most common forms of training in the industry is the apprenticeship, although it has different names in each country for the different levels you may be tackling. An apprenticeship usually leads to National Vocational Qualifications (NVQs or, in Scotland, SVQs) and the great advantage is that they enable you to earn as you learn. You are eligible to do an apprenticeship if you are between 16 and 24 years old and you have four GCSE passes.

- Apprenticeships in England, National Traineeships in Wales, or Modern Apprenticeships in Scotland (also sometimes known as Skillseekers) are equivalent to NVQ/SVQ level 1/2 and generally take a year and a half to two years to complete.
- The Advanced Apprenticeship in England, known as the Modern Apprenticeship in Wales and Scotland, is equivalent to NVQ/SVQ level 3 and usually takes at least an extra year to complete.

The skill levels in NVQ/SVQ terms can be broadly defined as:

● level 1 – basic skills, with an introduction to your chosen topic
● level 2 – completion of foundation skills
● level 3 – advanced skills, to give you specialist knowledge
● level 4 – supervisory skills, or very advanced technical skills
● level 5 – managerial skills for those who want to progress further.

You'll find that most of these apprenticeships are designed for school-leavers and young people. It is possible for more mature candidates to be accepted (as you'll see in the next section) but be prepared to discover that funding proves a little more difficult to get your hands on. Generally you have to complete your training qualifications by the age of 25.

There are five Key Skills: Communication, Numeracy, Information technology, Working with others and Problem solving.

An added bonus of studying for an apprenticeship will be that you also qualify in Key Skills. Called Core Skills in Scotland, these are rated as the skills that everyone needs to help them be successful in any industry or business. There are five Key Skills: communication, numeracy, information technology, working with others and problem solving.

The great advantage of these skills is that you can take them with you to whatever job you do, whether it's inside or outside the industry, and they will always be of value.

Construction Apprenticeship Scheme
There are many training schemes offered by the industry itself.
The Construction Apprenticeship Scheme (CAS) and the Scottish
Building Apprenticeship and Training Council (SBATC) run
programmes in conjunction with ConstructionSkills.

These will be run either by an employer or by an organisation that
works with employers to provide training. The programme
combines work experience and on-the-job training by
supervisors and training specialists with off-the-job training at a
college or training centre.

You will be helped to build up a National or Scottish Vocational
Qualification in all the necessary subjects at the right NVQ/SVQ
levels for your chosen career (usually a combination of levels 1, 2
and perhaps 3).

It normally takes between two and three years to achieve levels 1
and 2, and a further 18 months to reach level 3.

If you cannot find a position on a training course that suits you,
it might be possible to join a company, establish yourself in the
job and start your formal training later. ConstructionSkills can
help employers to find sponsorship funding for apprenticeships.

Once you have qualified in your chosen specialisation, you can
continue training to reach NVQ/SVQ levels 4 and 5 if you wish.
You can also take qualifications in related subjects, such as
welding and electrical installation, that have appropriate
NVQ/SVQ levels.

Unfortunately, there just aren't enough apprenticeships to go
round (ConstructionSkills estimates there are 34,000 people each
year who want to start an apprenticeship but can't find a place).

Because of this it has launched the Programme Led Apprenticeship which should have 3,000 places by 2008. This is a two-year, construction-based college course leading to an Intermediate Construction Award (ICA – see below for more detail). Having completed this, trainees can then go on to get a placement in the industry and work towards NVQ level 2 within 9 to 12 months.

CHARTERED INSTITUTE OF BUILDING (CIOB) STUDIES

If you are between 16 and 18 years old, you can become a student CIOB Member and study for full membership while you are working.

- level 1 – formation studies
- level 2 – core studies
- level 3 – professional studies (equivalent to a degree).

This programme can take up to six years, or even longer.

NATIONAL CONSTRUCTION COLLEGE

About 700 people each year go to the National Construction College (NCC), which is a network of colleges around the UK. The NCC offers courses in just about every aspect of construction work, mixing residential training with time spent doing jobs for companies on site.

HNC/HND

If you would like technical qualifications in construction and civil engineering, you could follow the Higher National Certificate (HNC) or Higher National Diploma (HND) programmes. If you are 16 and take the two-year part-time National Certificate (NC) course, you can progress to HNC; if you take the two-year full-time National Diploma (ND) course, you can progress to HND. Alternatively, if you are 18 and have A-levels, you can go straight onto an HNC or HND course.

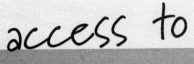

access to

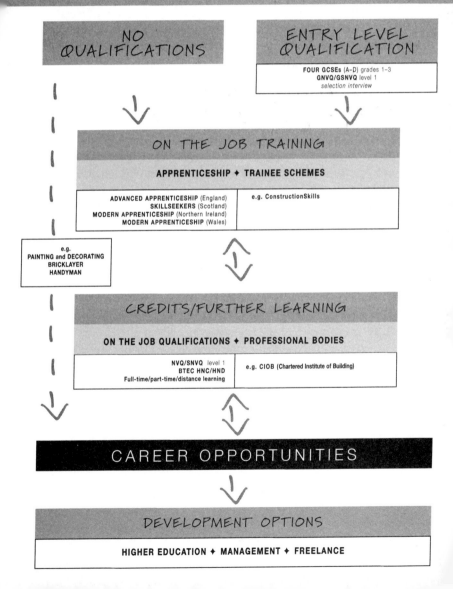

NO QUALIFICATIONS

ENTRY LEVEL QUALIFICATION

FOUR GCSEs (A–D) grades 1–3
GNVQ/GSNVQ level 1
selection interview

ON THE JOB TRAINING

APPRENTICESHIP ✦ TRAINEE SCHEMES

ADVANCED APPRENTICESHIP (England) **SKILLSEEKERS** (Scotland) **MODERN APPRENTICESHIP** (Northern Ireland) **MODERN APPRENTICESHIP** (Wales)	e.g. ConstructionSkills

e.g.
**PAINTING and DECORATING
BRICKLAYER
HANDYMAN**

CREDITS/FURTHER LEARNING

ON THE JOB QUALIFICATIONS ✦ PROFESSIONAL BODIES

NVQ/SNVQ level 1 **BTEC HNC/HND** Full-time/part-time/distance learning	e.g. CIOB (Chartered Institute of Building)

CAREER OPPORTUNITIES

DEVELOPMENT OPTIONS

HIGHER EDUCATION ✦ MANAGEMENT ✦ FREELANCE

The guide on the following page neatly sums up the various routes into the industry and shows how you can progress by getting more qualifications.

OTHER NEW INITIATIVES

Because the world of construction never stands still, with new technology and construction methods being introduced all the time, nor does the training. At present there are a number of new schemes being piloted across the country and they could be in place by the time you enter the industry.

Intermediate Construction Awards

The Construction Award is a new qualification that recognises the job knowledge and practical skills a person has gained during training. An Intermediate Construction Award (ICA) can be counted towards an NVQ at level 2. You can do an ICA in the following disciplines:

- accessing operations and rigging, scaffolding
- applied waterproof membrane, built up bituminous roofing
- construction and civil engineering services, construction operations
- construction and civil engineering services, highways maintenance (general highways operations)
- decorative occupations, painting and decorating
- floorcovering-textile and impervious
- formworking
- interior systems, dry lining
- maintenance operations
- mastic asphalting
- plant maintenance
- plastering
- roof sheeting and cladding
- roof slating and tiling
- stonemasonry
- thatching

- trowel occupations, bricklaying
- trowel occupations, craft mason
- wall and floor tiling
- wood occupations, bench joinery
- wood occupations, shopfitting (site work and bench work)
- wood occupations, site carpentry
- woodmachining

Specialised Diploma/GCSE

These new awards in construction and the built environment should be rolled out across the country by 2008 and will comprise a combination of:

- functional skills in maths, English and ICT; vocational, sector and occupationally specific learning; wider employability skills, and work experience
- the best of current qualifications including GCSEs and A-levels where appropriate, and will also include new content where employers identify need
- more opportunities to learn in a different, more adult environment, including the potential for experience in the workplace.

The GCSE can be taken as either a single or double award comprising core compulsory learning in 'the built environment and the construction industry' and 'design for sustainability and the built environment', together with one optional unit for the single award or three optional units for the double award. The technical and professional units are:

- building design
- construction processes and technology
- surveying

The craft-based units are:

- brickwork
- building services
- carpentry and joinery
- painting and decorating

Young Apprenticeships

If you are between 14 and 16 years old you can now do a Young Apprenticeship in Construction where you learn practical skills while still in full-time education. However, the Young Apprenticeships are still rolling out across the country and it is estimated that across all subjects only 9,000 pupils will start a Young Apprenticeship in September 2007.

City & Guilds/Baccalaureate

Still at the pilot stage is the City & Guilds level 2 Certificate in Construction Technology and the Built Environment, while a Construction Baccalaureate is still at the proposal stage. Talk to your careers advisor or contact your careers centre for the most up-to-date information on these new initiatives.

SPONSORSHIP

If you're lucky, you may get your studies paid for, either in full or in part. Many employers offer sponsorship to students choosing construction-related courses through their strong links with particular colleges and universities. The good news is that the employer will support you financially through your course and provide you with valuable hands-on work experience. What's more, you'll almost certainly be offered a job at the end of your

Don't forget to take advantage of the services offered by government-funded bodies such as Connexions and LearnDirect.

course. However, there is naturally a moral obligation to give good service to any employer who has treated you so well, which might have a restraining influence on your career. So think carefully about possible future plans before you accept.

FINDING A COURSE

Careers officers at school and general careers advisers should be able to point you in the right direction to find the course to suit your needs. Failing that, advisers at your local Jobcentre or employment agency will be able to recommend courses.

In certain areas, you may be eligible for the New Deal scheme (outlined below). Don't forget to take advantage of the services offered by government-funded bodies such as Connexions and LearnDirect.

You can do your own research on potential courses for the subject you want to study by checking in local phone books or the *Yellow Pages*. Several search engines on the Internet will also be able to give you details. As an alternative, the NVQ search on the ConstructionSkills website will help you to find a City & Guilds or ConstructionSkills accredited NVQ training provider in your area.

NEW DEAL

New Deal applies particularly in an area where job opportunities are limited. The scheme supports you if you're having difficulty in finding work by helping you get training towards a particular career. If you decide to participate in the scheme, you will have the support of a New Deal adviser who will help you to find a job and get the appropriate training. This training will normally lead to a part- or full-time NVQ. The New Deal scheme is administered by the Department of Work and Pensions. To find out the contact details of the service nearest to you, it's best to refer to your telephone directory or your local careers office.

HOW TO GET ACCEPTED ON A TRAINING PROGRAMME

There are five main ways of being taken on for training.

- You are nominated by a national training provider
- You are nominated by a local training provider
- You are nominated by a careers service/Connexions
- You are nominated by your local employment agency
- You are nominated by your employer.

All routes require you to take some action on your own behalf.

National training providers

Each country in the UK has a designated national training provider for the profession. These set out the overall plans and guidelines. ConstructionSkills is responsible for these guidelines in the UK and, in conjunction with various national bodies, forms these plans.

Local training providers

Each country in the UK is subdivided into smaller areas, where the advisers will know in greater detail what is happening in your area. Look at the Learning and Skills Councils for England, Scottish Enterprise and their local enterprise councils for Scotland and, in Wales, Education and Learning Wales.

Careers services

Both your local and your school careers services can refer you for training in the profession if you can demonstrate that you have the potential to succeed.

Connexions

Connexions is the government's support service for all young people between 13 and 19 years old in England. It can give you advice and help on starting your career and offer you personal development opportunities.

Local employment agency
Your Jobcentre or local employment agency can refer you for training in the profession. Again, you must show that you have the potential to succeed.

Employers
You can take the initiative and, if you are already in work, convince your employer to apply for you to receive training. Alternatively, you can approach prospective employers and undertake to carry out the training as a condition of employment.

In a way, there is no such thing as a typical career path in the construction industry. But, as you'll have gathered, there are three main ways to progress.

SUPERVISORY/MANAGERIAL

As you gain more knowledge and experience, there is often the chance to move into supervisory or managerial jobs. You can then receive the training you need to help you perform these roles – it's often quite a change from being one of the team to becoming the team leader.

DESIGN/PLANNING

Some of the planning, surveying, design and even technical support roles may become available to you and can represent career progression if you've shown an aptitude for this type of work. Obviously these jobs will only suit those who are quite happy with a high percentage of deskbound work.

RUNNING YOUR OWN BUSINESS

There are opportunities to set up a business in most construction skills areas. But you must be prepared for all the extra paperwork that managing your own company will undoubtedly cause, not to mention the special problems involved in employing people to work for you (if you choose to expand).

The best thing to do is to ask someone you know who has set up their own business, take their advice about the potential benefits and pitfalls, and make your own decision about whether you want to make this one of your aims.

STUDENT EXPERIENCES

Here are some thoughts from four construction students at South Thames College.

Matt Hunt, 23 years old, ConstructionSkills/City & Guilds in Bench Joinery

'I was at college doing something else for a year and then I left and went out to work in the construction industry for two years. My grandfather and other relatives have been carpenters and I just like working with my hands so I decided to do this course. This is definitely what I want to do as a career and once I've finished this course I'm going to go out and work as a carpenter. I'm already doing some general building work because I think being successful in this career is as much about having experience as anything else. I do think carpenters are valued for the skills we have by the people who employ us because we can do something they can't do for themselves.'

Jenne Blake, 37 years old, also doing Bench Joinery

'I have three children, but am a single parent and I wanted to be able to do building jobs around the house myself. However, I'm also doing this course because I'd like to do carpentry as a career if I'm any good at it! In fact, I'd also like to do other courses such as plastering and plumbing. I've never done anything practical before as my background is actually in graphic design, so I'm finding it quite difficult but also very interesting. Ultimately, I'd like to become an apprentice and learn more on the job.'

Tim Shbetim, 26 years old, Bench Joinery and ConstructionSkills/City & Guilds Hot and Cold Water (Plumbing)

'I'm doing these courses for the qualifications because having accredited qualifications proves to people you really are a trained carpenter or a trained plumber. I'm doing two courses because I think it is good to have more than one skill in fact I think it is good to have more than two skills so I'm thinking of doing an electrician's course as well. These are skills I will have all my life, whatever else I decide to do.'

Simon Williams, 47 years old, also doing Bench Joinery and Hot and Cold Water (Plumbing)

'I'm of the generation where we all thought we would have a job for life, whereas nowadays it is not unusual to have three different careers in your life. Many people of my age want to go out and actually make something rather than be sitting in front of a computer and having these skills means I can choose whether to work alone as a freelancer or to work within a group of people on larger projects.'

9

Getting a job

Getting a job anywhere always demands that you follow a certain set of guidelines and in this chapter there are some clues on how to look and how to act as well as what potential employers might be expecting to hear.

It's best to be thorough and methodical in your attempts to find a possible employer. For instance, it might be a good idea to start in your local town or area. If that draws a blank, then spread the net to bring in adjacent towns and areas – and go on broadening your approach until you get a favourable response.

The important point is that you must not get downcast by people turning you away. The job market is highly competitive and employers receive many applications for each position (that's if they're even taking people on), so you must not take any rejections personally. Eventually your persistence will bear fruit.

It's a good idea to review constantly the way that your message is coming across to possible employers. Your character and personality cannot register with them until they've seen you. Bear in mind you've got to convince people to grant you an interview in the first place. In the next section, there are some suggestions on how best to present yourself on paper – how to write a CV and compose a letter to go with it.

WORK EXPERIENCE

There's nothing that demonstrates your commitment so well as doing a trial period in the industry (and preferably with the company you want to join). First of all, there's no better way to test the waters than to gain real work experience. Construction offers a huge variety of two-week placements to help you decide if it's the right career for you. Most schools run work experience schemes and may be able to arrange one for you.

There's nothing that demonstrates your commitment so well as doing a trial period in the industry.

If you enjoy your work experience, and all goes well, then you'll have a head start when you come to apply for a job. Even if things haven't gone so smoothly, you'll still have gained valuable knowledge – and you can explain that you'll put your learning to good use in the future. Companies don't expect perfection from someone on a work experience placement. It's attitude that counts.

MAKE THE MOST OF YOURSELF

Here are a few suggestions about presenting yourself on paper to potential employers – how to write an eye-catching CV and a punchy covering letter.

Remember what the function of a CV is: to make you stand out from the crowd and get you an interview. So keep it short – no more than two pages – but provide employers with the sort of detail that will bring you to their notice.

Lay out your CV neatly and clearly, whether it is being sent by post or email. Check carefully to make sure everything reads well and that there are no mistakes.

DID YOU KNOW?

In June 2007 the new Peninsula Square was opened in Greenwich, London. It is linked to the O2 Arena (formerly the Dome) by a 590 ft canopy, and has a 147 ft steel spire, and an impressive bank of water features. Builders also installed the largest area of natural stone paving in London, covering 43,000 sq ft, which is the size of Leicester Square.

Compose your covering letter with great care so that it conveys your enthusiasm for joining the company without indulging in overselling.

For a full examination of how to present yourself on paper, try *Winning CVs for First-Time Job Hunters* by Kathleen Houston (Trotman) which has excellent advice on every stage of the process.

This is an industry with real opportunities for advancement. As you go through the training and discover where your strengths lie, you will be able to map out your future career path. The diagram below shows options that will open up to you once you have trained.

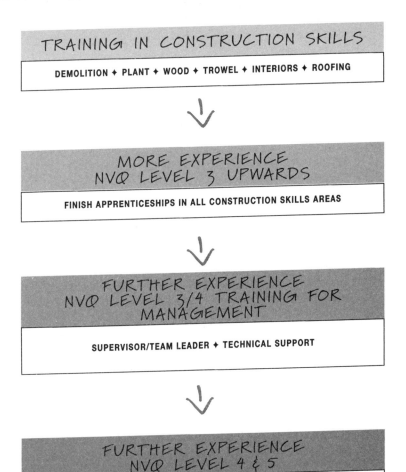

TRAINING IN CONSTRUCTION SKILLS

DEMOLITION ✦ PLANT ✦ WOOD ✦ TROWEL ✦ INTERIORS ✦ ROOFING

MORE EXPERIENCE
NVQ LEVEL 3 UPWARDS

FINISH APPRENTICESHIPS IN ALL CONSTRUCTION SKILLS AREAS

FURTHER EXPERIENCE
NVQ LEVEL 3/4 TRAINING FOR MANAGEMENT

SUPERVISOR/TEAM LEADER ✦ TECHNICAL SUPPORT

FURTHER EXPERIENCE
NVQ LEVEL 4 & 5

FOREMAN/SITE MANAGER ✦ DESIGN
PLANNING ✦ MANAGEMENT

10 The last word

Twenty years ago the thought of a TV character called Bob The Builder becoming a household name and a role model for young children would have made most people laugh out loud. But times change and so has the construction business and our perception of the people who work in it. It is now a thriving, exciting and creative industry, transforming our environment and offering real benefits for those who choose to make a career in it.

There has never been a better time to train in construction, not only because there is an urgent need for well-qualified professionals in all areas, but also because the industry has taken massive strides in providing good-quality training programmes. Once trained you will enter a world of work that can be hard, both physically and mentally, but offers great rewards in being creative, practical and above all fulfilling.

Many builders, especially those who have worked on architecturally interesting structures, are more than happy to point them out to you and discuss in detail 'their bits', the areas they worked on. They take great pride in what they have achieved and these days the monetary rewards for their work can be substantial.

This is an industry where there is huge scope for you to advance to managerial levels or even to end up running your own business. The future for the construction industry is looking bright and hopefully this book has helped you to make up your mind if you want to be a part of it. The following chapter contains the names and addresses of the organisations that can help you if you want to make a career in construction a reality.

If you have made it this far through the book then you should know if **construction** really is the career for you. But, before contacting the professional bodies listed in the next chapter, here's a final, fun checklist to show if you have chosen wisely.

THE LAST WORD

DO YOU LIKE WORKING WITH YOUR HANDS?
☐ YES
☐ NO

DO YOU LIKE WORKING WITH PEOPLE?
☐ YES
☐ NO

DO YOU CONSIDER YOURSELF CREATIVE?
☐ YES
☐ NO

DO YOU WANT A JOB WHERE YOU WILL BE DOING SOMETHING DIFFERENT EVERY DAY?
☐ YES
☐ NO

ARE YOU SELF-MOTIVATED AND ABLE TO THINK ON YOUR FEET?
☐ YES
☐ NO

ARE YOU ABLE TO COMMUNICATE EFFECTIVELY WITH LOTS OF DIFFERENT PEOPLE?
☐ YES
☐ NO

ARE YOU A SELF STARTER, ABLE TO TAKE CONTROL AND RESPONSIBILITY?
☐ YES
☐ NO

If you answered 'YES' to all these questions then
CONGRATULATIONS! YOU'VE CHOSEN THE RIGHT CAREER!

If you answered 'NO' to any of these questions then this may not be the career for you.
However, there are still some options open to you.

For example you could work as a sales person at a builders merchant or DIY store

Further information

In this section are the addresses, telephone numbers and websites of organisations that can help you to get your first job in construction or to find the right training course.

Chartered Institute of Building (CIOB)
Englemere
Kings Ride
Ascot
Berkshire
SL5 7TB
01344 630700
www.ciob.org.uk

This is the leading professional body for managers in the construction industry and has more than 42,000 members worldwide. The website includes an industry education section.

ConstructionSkills (formerly Construction Industry Training Board (CITB))
Bircham Newton
Kings Lynn
Norfolk
PE31 6RH
01485 577577
www.constructionskills.net

ConstructionSkills works in partnership with CITB Northern Ireland and the Construction Industry Council (CIC) as the Sector Skills Council for construction skills. It runs most of the employer-based training for the construction industry in the UK and is committed to training professionals to a very high level. If you wish to get a place on its Construction Apprenticeship Scheme, you can apply to ConstructionSkills direct. It publishes some very informative pamphlets and brochures. Alternatively, look at the careers section of the website.

National Construction College (NCC)
0870 416 6222
www.constructionskills.net

The NCC is a network of colleges around the country that specialise in training young people as skilled operatives and potential supervisors in the construction industry. All courses combine a mixture of site work and residential training and last between four and 43 weeks.

Engineering Construction Industry Training Board (ECITB)
Blue Court
Church Lane
Kings Langley
Herts
WD4 8JP
01923 260000
www.ecitb.org.uk

Look under industry and careers and also learning and development on the ECITB website for relevant information. The website also contains a list of upcoming careers exhibitions across the country.

Glass and Glazing Federation (GGF)
44–48 Borough High Street
London
SE1 1XB
0870 042 4266
www.ggf.co.uk

This trade association for those who make, supply or fit flat glass provides extensive information about the industry.

The Institute of Plumbing and Heating Engineering (IPHE)
64 Station Lane
Hornchurch
Essex
RM12 6NB
01708 472791
www.iphe.org.uk

Founded in 1906, this is the professional body for plumbers and others in the plumbing industry. It has an extensive Career Zone.

Institution of Civil Engineers (ICE)
1 Great George Street
London
SW1P 3AA
020 7222 7722
www.ice.org.uk

The ICE website gives information, the latest news about civil engineering and debates current issues, such as the lack of women in the industry.

Painting & Decorating Association (PDA)

32 Coton Road
Nuneaton
Warwicks
CV11 5TW
024 7635 3776
www.paintingdecoratingassociation.co.uk

This is the largest organisation in the UK catering exclusively for the needs of the painter and decorator.

Royal Institute of British Architects (RIBA)

66 Portland Place
London
W1B 1AD
020 7580 5533
www.riba.org
www.architecture.com

The RIBA website is the world's most extensive built-environment careers portal, with news, views and masses of information.

Royal Institution of Chartered Surveyors (RICS)

RICS Contact Centre
Surveyor Court
Westwood Way
Coventry
CV4 8JE
0870 333 1600
www.rics.org

The RICS website is aimed at property professionals and has an excellent Career Zone.

TRAINING PROVIDERS AND ADVISERS

City & Guilds
1 Giltspur Street
London
EC1A 9DD
020 7294 2800
www.city-and-guilds.co.uk

City & Guilds is the leading provider of vocational qualifications in the United Kingdom. It offers everything from NVQ and SVQ to Apprenticeships and Higher Level Qualifications. The excellent website lists all the qualifications it provides in construction.

Connexions
www.connexions-direct.com

The Connexions service has been set up especially for 13 to 19-year-olds and offers advice, support and practical help on many subjects, including your future career options. Check out the Jobs4u career database.

CAREER DEVELOPMENT LOANS
Packs available by calling 0800 585505
www.direct.gov.uk

If you are undertaking a vocational training course lasting up to two years (including one year's practical work experience if it is part of the course), you may be eligible for a Career Development Loan. These are available for full-time, part-time and distance learning courses and applicants can be employed, self-employed or unemployed. The DfES pays interest on the loan for the length of the course and up to one month afterwards.

SORT IT OUT!

HOW DO I KNOW WHICH JOBS ARE RIGHT FOR ME?

No problem, you can log onto **cityandguilds.com/myperfectjob** and take 20 minutes to answer a range of online questions which looks at your interests, personality and lifestyle and suggests job areas which may suit you. Get all the information on job options, how to get started and where you can go to study.
cityandguilds.com/myperfectjob

Edexcel
One90 High Holborn
London
WC1V 7BH
0870 240 9800
www.edexcel.org.uk

Edexcel has taken over from BTEC in offering BTEC
qualifications, including BTEC First Diplomas, BTEC National
Diplomas and BTEC Higher Nationals (HNC and HND). It also
offers NVQ qualifications.

The website includes qualification 'quick links' and you can
search either by the qualification or the career in which you are
interested.

Learning and Skills Council
Apprenticeship helpline: 08000 150 600
www.apprenticeships.org.uk

The Learning and Skills Council is responsible for the largest
investment in post-16 education and training in England. It is also
responsible for the planning and funding of all post-16 education
outside higher education. It has a budget of £10.4 billion for
2007 and there are currently 259,000 apprentices working in
over 130,000 businesses.

For MAs in Scotland
0845 850 2502
www.scottish-enterprise.com/modern-apprenticeships

For MAs in Wales
029 2090 6801
www.careerswales.com

For Apprenticeships in Northern Ireland
0800 100 900

Much of the Learning and Skills Council website is still being developed.

Its realworkrealpay website is specifically aimed at those who would like to do an apprenticeship.

In Scotland
www.modernapprenticeships.com
www.careers.scotland.org.uk

In Wales
www.beskilled.net

New Deal
0845 606 2626
www.newdeal.co.uk

The New Deal applies particularly in areas where job opportunities are limited. The scheme supports you if you're having difficulty in finding work by helping you to get training towards a particular career.

New Deal also has a Jobseeker Direct helpline on 0845 606 0234.

Qualifications and Curriculum Authority (QCA)
83 Piccadilly
London
W1J 8QA
020 7509 5555
www.qca.org.uk

Scottish Qualifications Authority (SQA)
The Optima Building
58 Robertson Street
Glasgow
G2 8DQ
0845 279 1000
www.sqa.org.uk

These official awarding bodies will be able to tell you whether the course you choose leads to a nationally approved qualification such as NVQ or SVQ.

PERIODICALS
Construction Magazine
7 Bay Hall
Willow Lane
Birkby
Huddersfield
HD1 5EN
01484 321000
enquiries@planet-group.co.uk

This monthly magazine has news on projects and company features and is aimed at the general construction industry.

Building
The Builder Group
Ludgate House
245 Blackfriars Road
London
SE1 9UY
020 7921 5000
www.building.co.uk

Launched way back in 1843, *Building* is the oldest weekly construction title, with over 100,000 readers. It is a mine of